more of...

T0120929

All the tunes you've ever wanted to play!

Easy-to-play Piano Arrangements

Order No. AM 981387
International Standard Book Number: 0.8256.2996.9

Exclusive Distributors:
Music Sales Corporation
257 Park Avenue South, New York, NY 10010 USA
Music Sales Limited
8/9 Frith Street, London W1D 3JB England
Music Sales Pty. Limited
120 Rothschild Street, Rosebery, Sydney, NSW 2018, Australia

Printed in the United States of America by
Vicks Lithograph and Printing Corporation

633 SQUADRON MARCH

Ron Goodwin

Tempo alla Marcia (♩. = 116)

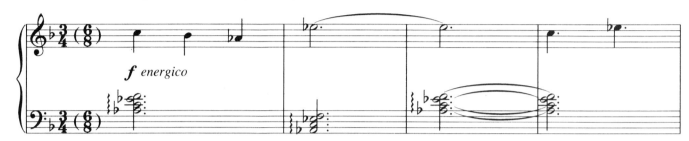

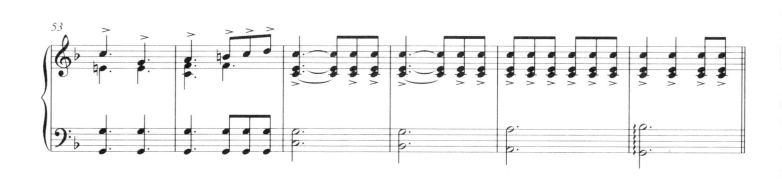

come primo

sim.

A-TISKET, A-TASKET

Traditional

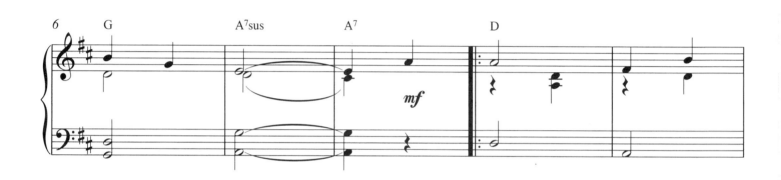

AMERICAN BEAUTY
(from "American Beauty")
Music by Thomas Newman

Moderately

AMAZING GRACE

Traditional

ANGEL EYES

Words by Earl Brent
Music by Matt Dennis

16

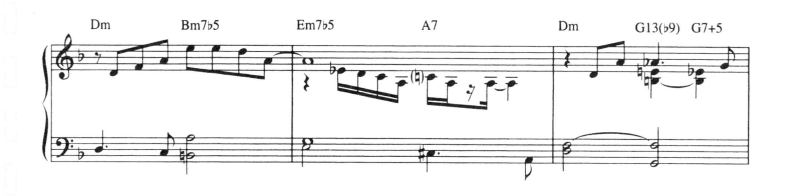

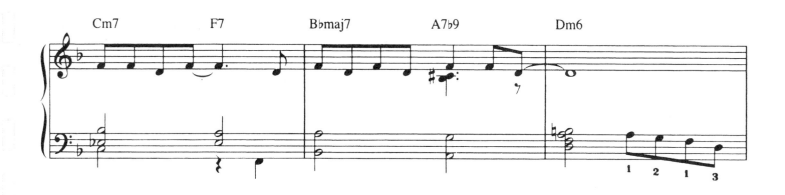

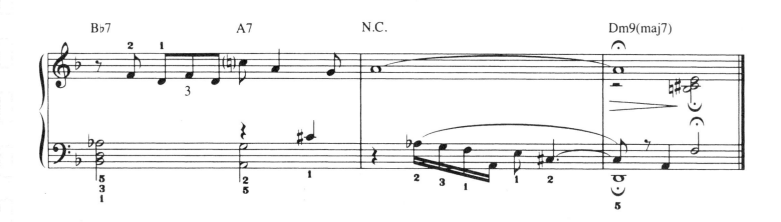

AQUARIUM
(from "The Carnival Of Animals")
By Camille Saint-Saëns

AS TIME GOES BY

Words and Music by Herman Hupfeld

22

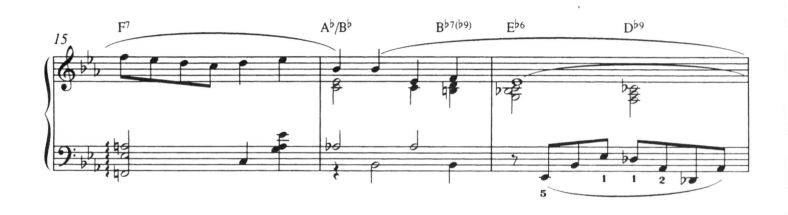

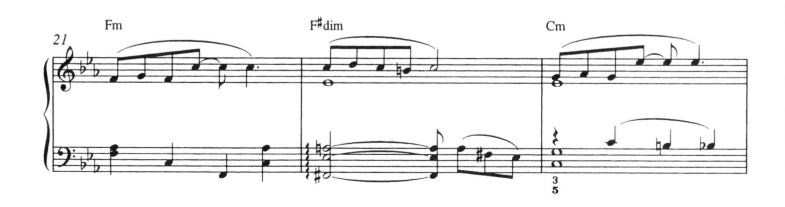

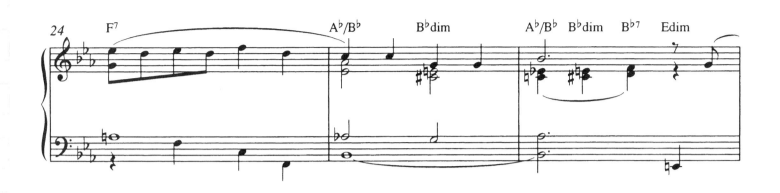

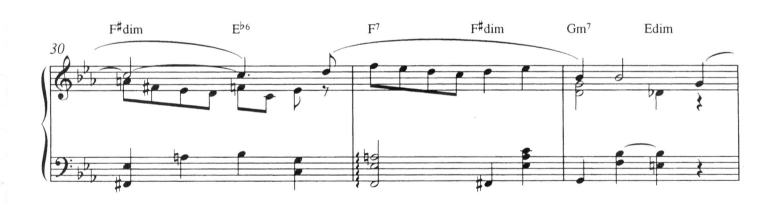

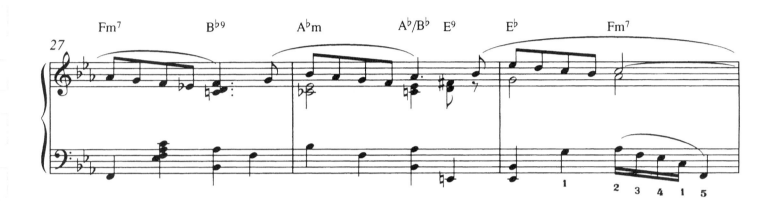

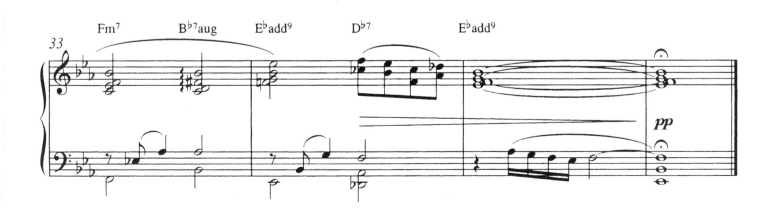

ARIA
(from "Goldberg Variations")
Johann Sebastian Bach

Adagio (♩ = 66)

THE ARRIVAL OF THE QUEEN OF SHEBA

(from "Solomon")

George Frideric Handel

THE ASHOKAN FAREWELL
(from the TV series "The Civil War")
By Jay Ungar

Freely, with expression

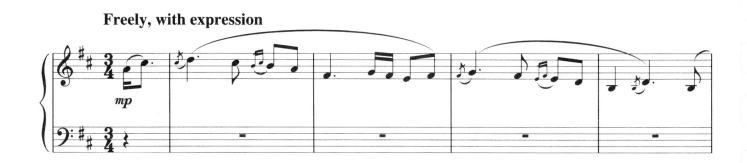

a tempo (but still a little freely) ♩ = *c*.88

AULD LANG SYNE

Traditional Scottish/Words by Robert Burns

Andante con moto

AWAY IN A MANGER

Traditional/Music by William Kirkpatrick

2. The cattle are lowing, the baby awakes,
   But little Lord Jesus no crying he makes,
   I love thee, Lord Jesus, look down from the sky,
   And stay by my side until morning is nigh.

3. Be near me, Lord Jesus, I ask thee to stay
   Close by me for ever, and love me, I pray:
   Bless all the dear children in thy tender care,
   And fit us for heaven, to live with thee there.

AVE VERUM CORPUS IN D MAJOR
(K.618)
Wolfgang Amadeus Mozart

BAGATELLE IN G MINOR
(Op. 119, No. 1)
Ludwig van Beethoven

42

THE BEGINNING OF THE PARTNERSHIP

(from "Shakespeare In Love")

Composed by Stephen Warbeck

BETWEEN THE DEVIL AND THE DEEP BLUE SEA

(From "Rhythmania")

Lyric by Ted Koehler
Music by Harold Arlen

48

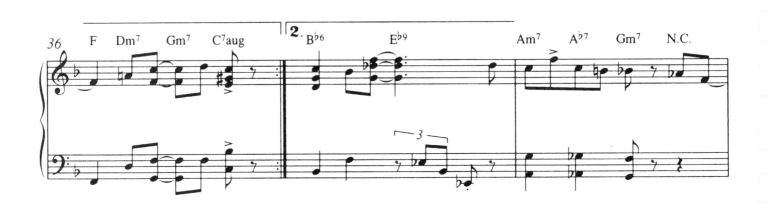

BIG SPENDER

(from "Sweet Charity")

Music by CY COLEMAN
Lyric by DOROTHY FIELDS

Aggressively, with swing

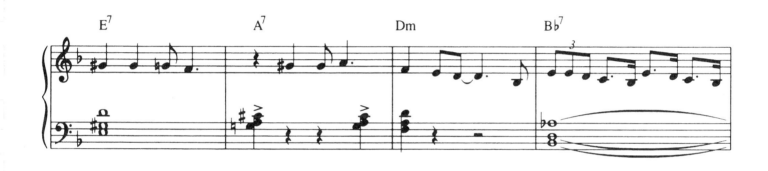

BLOW THE MAN DOWN

Traditional

COVENTRY CAROL

Traditional

2. Herod, the king,
   In his raging,
     Chargèd he hath this day
   His men of might,
   In his own sight,
     All young childrén to slay.

3. That woe is me,
   Poor child for thee!
     And ever morn and day,
   For thy parting
   Neither say nor sing
     By by, lully, lullay!

BRIDGE OVER TROUBLED WATER

Words and Music by Paul Simon

Moderato, not too fast, like a spiritual

58

CANDLE IN THE WIND

Words and Music by ELTON JOHN & BERNIE TAUPIN

In a slow 2

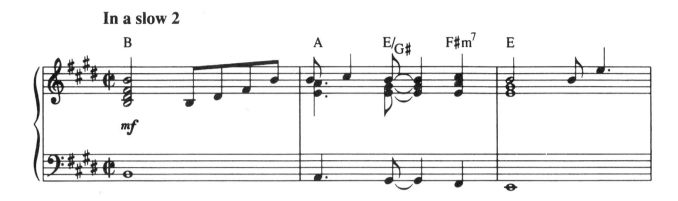

60

CASTA DIVA
(from "Norma")
By Vincenzo Bellini

Andante sostenuto (♩. = 50)

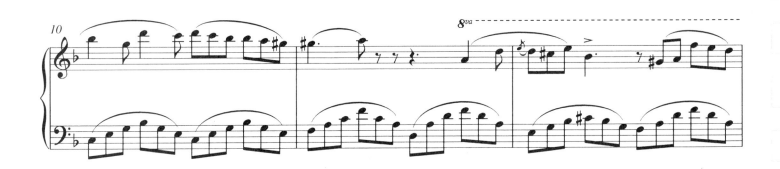

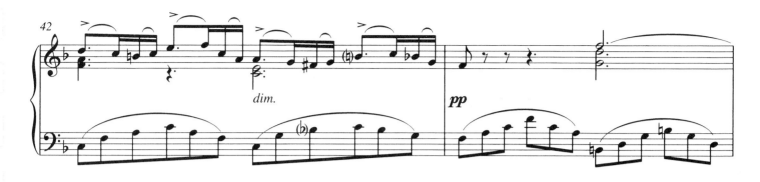

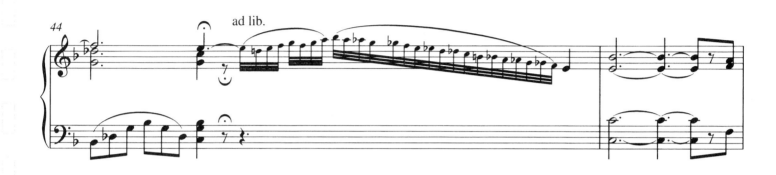

(THEY LONG TO BE) CLOSE TO YOU

Words by HAL DAVID
Music by BURT BACHARACH

Slowly and steady

COME WHAT MAY
(from the Motion Picture "Moulin Rouge")
Words and Music by DAVID BAERWALD

71

DECK THE HALLS

Traditional

2. See the blazing Yule before us,
   Fa-la-la-la-la, la-la-la-la.
   Strike the harp and join the chorus,
   Fa-la-la-la-la, la-la-la-la.
   Follow me in merry measure,
   Fa-la-la; la-la-la; la-la-la.
   While I tell of Yuletide treasure,
   Fa-la-la-la-la, la-la-la-la.

3. Fast away the old year passes,
   Fa-la-la-la-la, la-la-la-la.
   Hail the new, ye lads and lasses,
   Fa-la-la-la-la, la-la-la-la.
   Sing we joyous all together,
   Fa-la-la; la-la-la; la-la-la.
   Heedless of the wind and weather.
   Fa-la-la-la-la, la-la-la-la.

LA CUCARACHA

Traditional Mexican

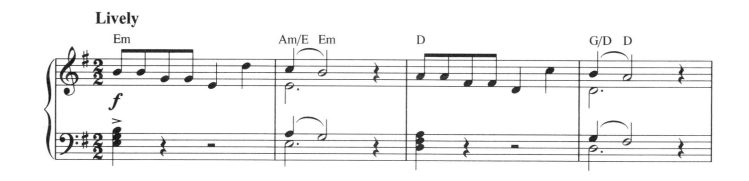

DING DONG! MERRILY ON HIGH

Words by George Woodard
Music: Traditional

Ding dong! mer-ri-ly on high____ in heav'n the bells are ring - ing:
Ding dong! ve-ri-ly the sky____ is riv'n with An - gels sing - ing.

Glo - - - - - - - - - - - ri-a, Ho-san-na in ex - cel - sis!

2. E'en so here below, below,
   Let steeple bells be swungen,
   And *i-o, i-o, i-o,*
   By priest and people sungen.
   Gloria, Hosanna in excelsis!

3. Pray you, dutifully prime
   Your Matin chime, ye ringers;
   May you beautifully rime
   Your Evetime Song, ye singers:
   Gloria, Hosanna in excelsis!

DON'T CRY FOR ME ARGENTINA

(from "Evita")

Music by ANDREW LLOYD WEBBER
Words by TIM RICE

78

DRINK TO ME ONLY WITH THINE EYES

Traditional English/Words by Benjamin Jonson

EL CONDOR PASA (IF I COULD)

Traditional South American

THE ENTERTAINER

(from the film "The Sting")

By Scott Joplin

ETERNAL FLAME

Words and Music by BILLY STEINBERG, TOM KELLY and SUSANNA HOFFS

90

92

FRANKIE AND JOHNNY
Traditional African-American

With feeling

THE ETERNAL VOW
(from the Motion Picture "Crouching Tiger, Hidden Dragon"
Composed by Tan Dun

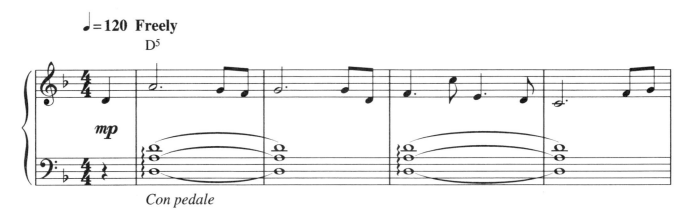

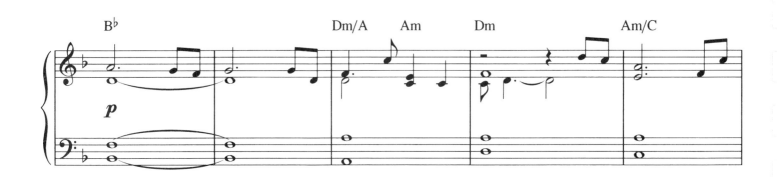

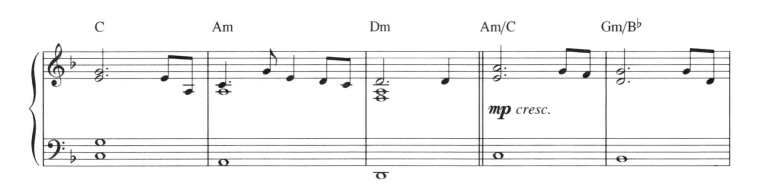

(EVERYTHING I DO) I DO IT FOR YOU

(from the Motion Picture "Robin Hood: Prince of Thieves")

Words and Music by BRYAN ADAMS, ROBERT JOHN LANGE and MICHAEL KAMEN

Slowly

THE FIRST NOËL

Traditional

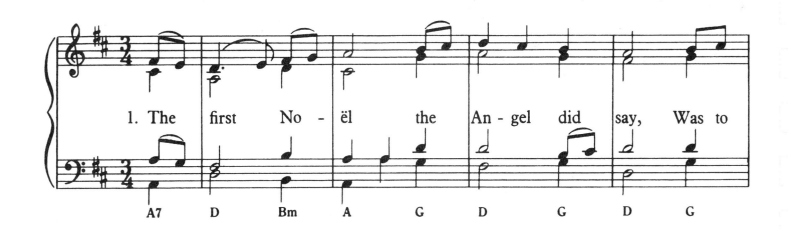

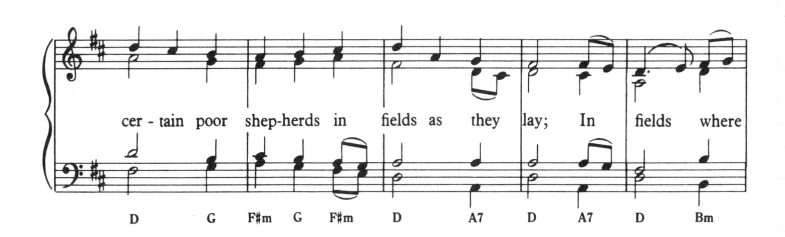

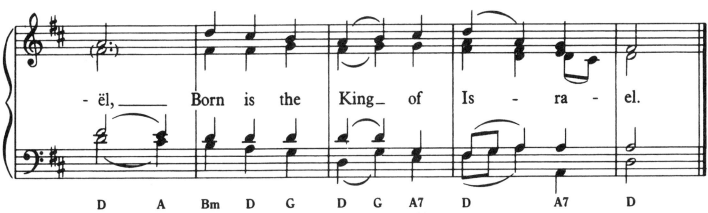

2. They lookèd up and saw a Star,
   Shining in the East, beyond them far,
   And to the earth it gave great light,
   And so it continued both day and night.
   Noël, etc.

3. And by the light of that same Star,
   Three Wise Men came from country far;
   To seek for a King was their intent,
   And to follow the Star wherever it went.
   Noël, etc.

4. This star drew nigh to the north-west,
   O'er Bethlehem it took its rest,
   And there it did both stop and stay,
   Right over the place where Jesus lay.
   Noël, etc.

5. Then entered in those Wise Men three,
   Full reverently upon their knee,
   And offered there, in His Presence,
   Their gold, and myrrh, and frankincense.
   Noël, etc.

6. Then let us all with one accord,
   Sing praises to our Heavenly Lord,
   That hath made Heaven and earth of nought,
   And with His Blood mankind hath bought.
   Noël, etc.

THE FLOWER DUET

(from "Lakme")

Music by Leo Delibes

Text by Edmond Gondinet & Philippe Gille

Andantino con moto (♪ = 118)

FLY ME TO THE MOON (IN OTHER WORDS)

Words and Music by Bart Howard

THE GIRL FROM IPANEMA
(GAROTA DE IPANEMA)

Music by ANTONIO CARLOS JOBIM
Original Words by VINICIUS DE MORAES
English Words by NORMAN GIMBEL

Moderately

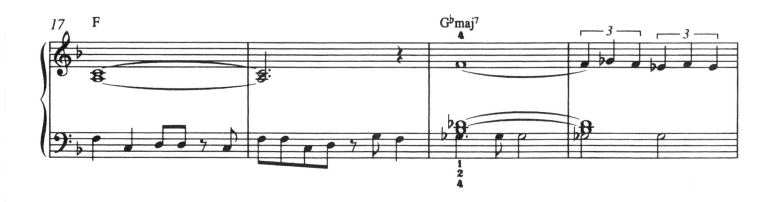

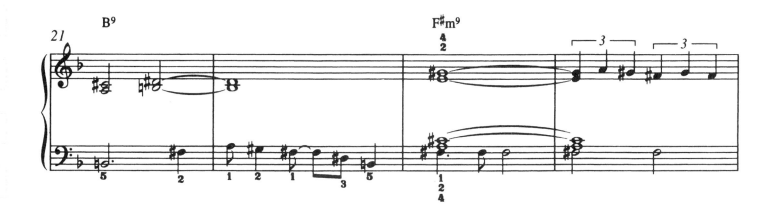

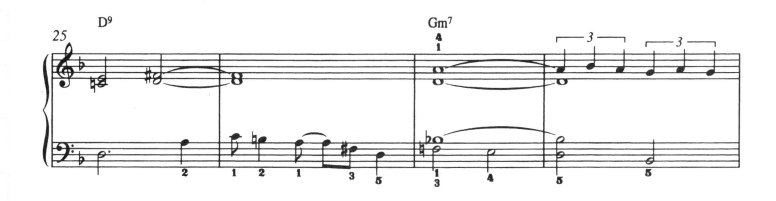

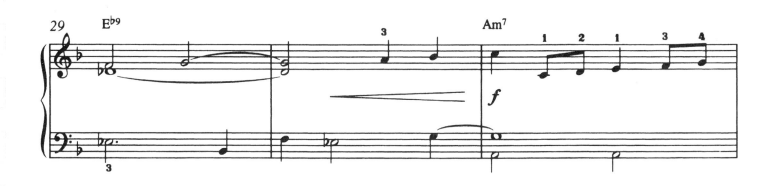

108

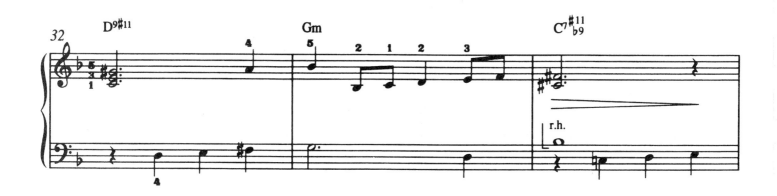

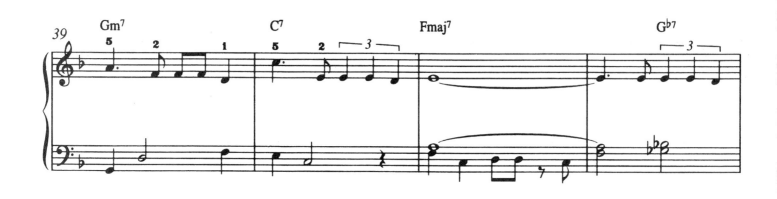

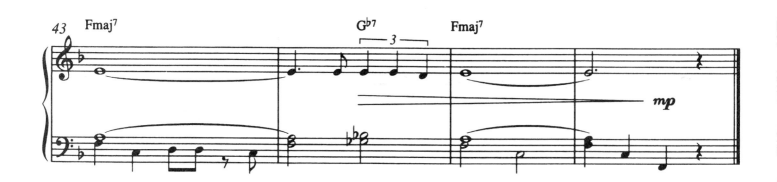

GO TELL IT ON THE MOUNTAIN

Traditional African-American

GOD REST YE MERRY, GENTLEMEN

Traditional

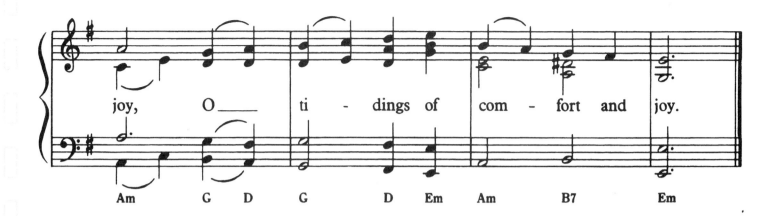

joy,   O___ ti - dings of com - fort and joy.

Am   G   D   G   D Em Am   B7   Em

2. In Bethlehem, in Jewry,
   This blessèd Babe was born,
And laid within a manger,
   Upon this blessèd morn;
The which His Mother Mary
   Did nothing take in scorn.
      O tidings, etc.

3. From God our Heavenly Father
   A blessed Angel came;
And unto certain Shepherds
   Brought tidings of the same:
How that in Bethlehem was born
   The Son of God by name.
      O tidings, etc.

4. "Fear not then," said the Angel,
   "Let nothing you affright,
This day is born a Saviour
   Of a pure Virgin bright,
To free all those that trust in Him
   From Satan's power and might."
      O tidings, etc.

5. The shepherds at those tidings
   Rejoicèd much in mind,
And left their flocks a-feeding,
   In tempest, storm, and wind:
And went to Bethlehem straightway,
   The Son of God to find.
      O tidings, etc.

6. And when they came to Bethlehem
   Where our dear Saviour lay,
They found Him in a manger,
   Where oxen fed on hay;
His Mother Mary kneeling down,
   Unto the Lord did pray.
      O tidings, etc.

7. Now to the Lord sing praises,
   All you within this place,
And with true love and brotherhood
   Each other now embrace;
This holy tide of Christmas
   All other do deface.
      O tidings, etc.

HERE'S THAT RAINY DAY

Words and Music by Johnny Burke and Jimmy Van Heusen

114

GREENSLEEVES

Traditional English

HARK! THE HERALD ANGELS SING

Music by Felix Mendelssohn
Words by Charles Wesley

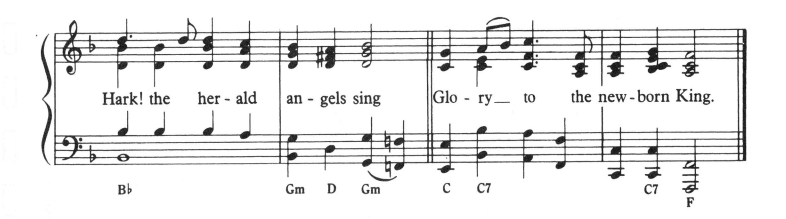

2. Christ, by highest heaven adored,
   Christ, the everlasting Lord,
   Late in time behold him come,
   Offspring of a Virgin's womb,
   Veiled in flesh the Godhead see!
   Hail, the incarnate Deity!
   Pleased as Man with man to dwell,
   Jesus, our Emmanuel.
       Hark! the herald angels sing
       Glory to the new-born King.

3. Hail, the heaven-born Prince of Peace!
   Hail, the Sun of Righteousness,
   Light and life to all he brings,
   Risen with healing in his wings.
   Mild he lays his glory by,
   Born that man no more may die,
   Born to raise the sons of earth,
   Born to give them second birth.
       Hark! the herald angels sing
       Glory to the new-born King.

HAVAH NAGILAH

Traditional Israeli

HE AIN'T HEAVY, HE'S MY BROTHER

Words by Bob Russell
Music by Bobby Scott

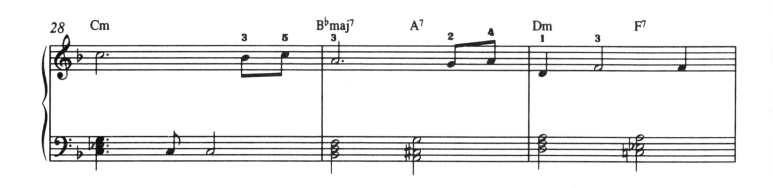

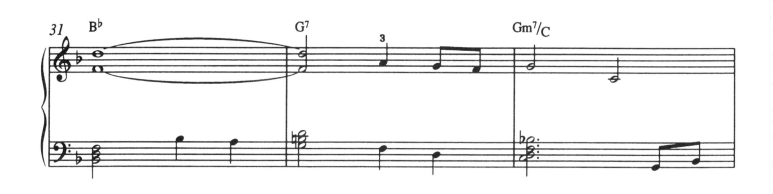

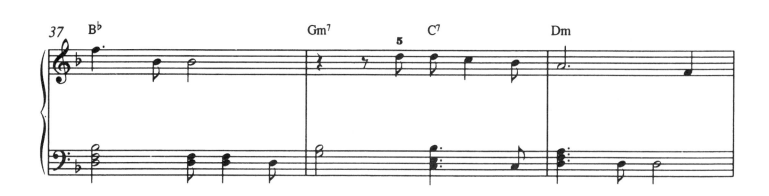

123

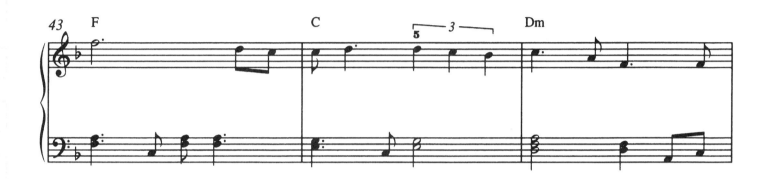

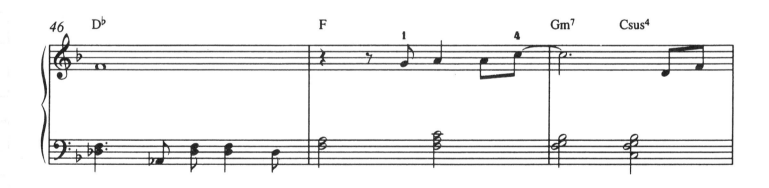

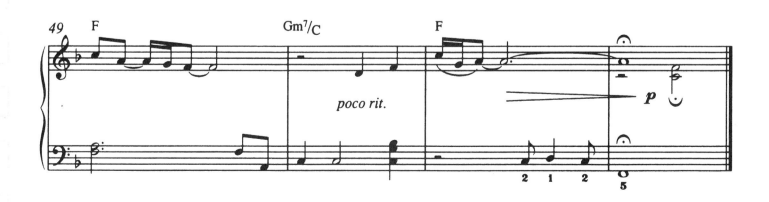

THE HOLLY AND THE IVY

Traditional

3. The holly bears a berry
   As red as any blood,
   And Mary bore sweet Jesus Christ,
   To do poor sinners good:
     Refrain:

4. The holly bears a prickle,
   As sharp as any thorn,
   And Mary bore sweet Jesus Christ
   On Christmas day in the morn:
     Refrain:

I SAW THREE SHIPS

Traditional

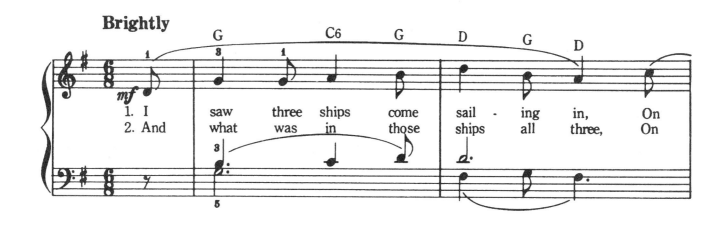

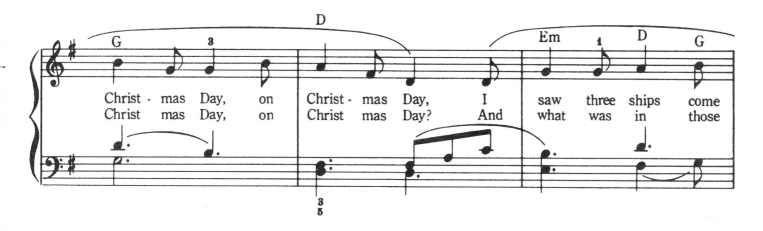

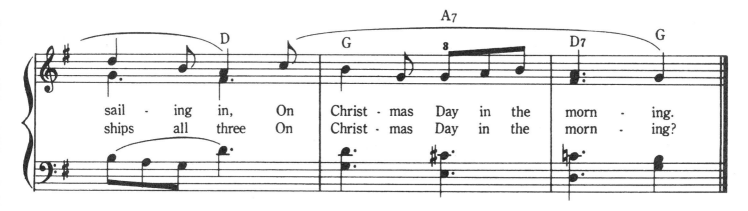

3. The Virgin Mary and Christ was there,
   On Christmas Day, on Christmas Day.
   The Virgin Mary and Christ was there,
   On Christmas Day in the morning.

4. Then let us all rejoice amain,
   On Christmas Day, on Christmas Day,
   Then let us all rejoice amain,
   On Christmas day in the morning.

HOME ON THE RANGE

Words by Brewster M. Higley
Music by Daniel E. Kelly

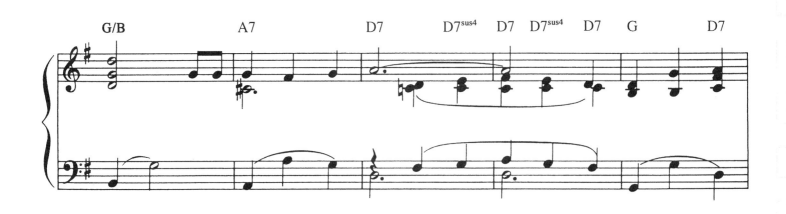

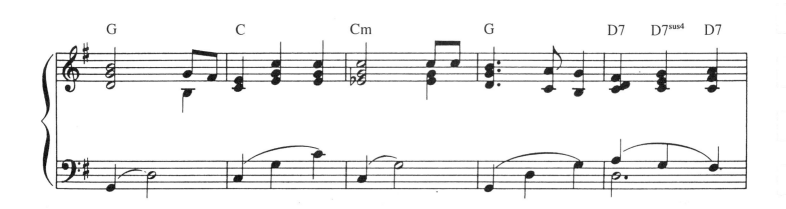

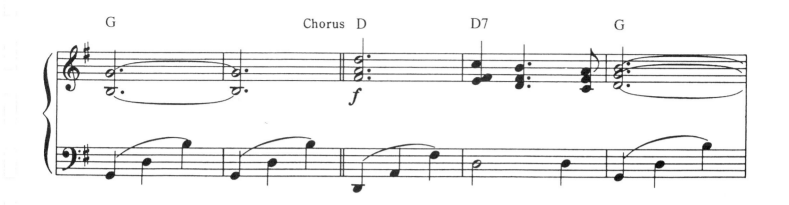

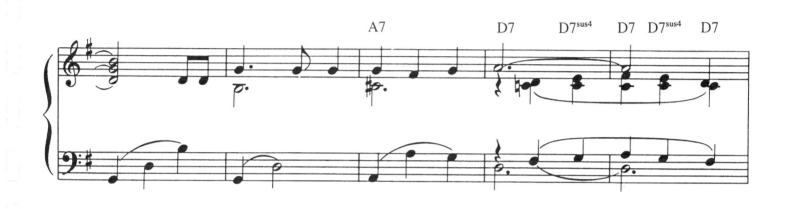

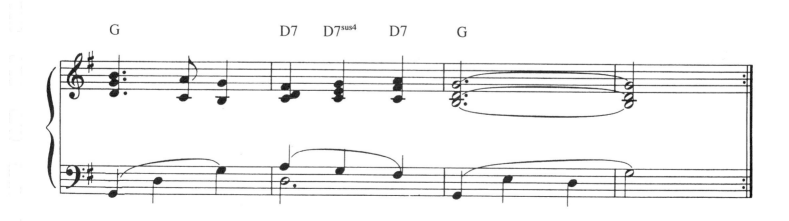

I KNOW HIM SO WELL

Words and Music by BENNY ANDERSSON, TIM RICE and BJORN ULVAEUS

HOW DEEP IS YOUR LOVE

(from the Motion Picture "Saturday Night Fever")

Words and Music by Barry Gibb, Maurice Gibb and Robin Gibb

I WILL ALWAYS LOVE YOU

Words and Music by DOLLY PARTON

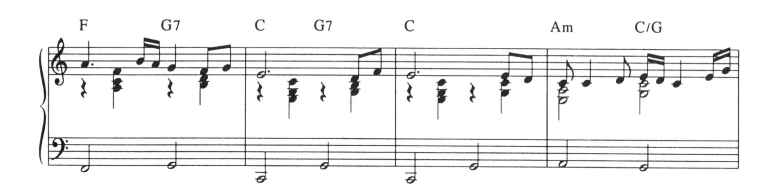

IS YOU IS, OR IS YOU AIN'T (MA' BABY?)

(from "Five Guys Named Moe")

Words and Music by BILLY AUSTIN and LOUIS JORDAN

139

LA MARSEILLAISE
(The French National Anthem)
Music by Claude Joseph Rouget de L'Isle

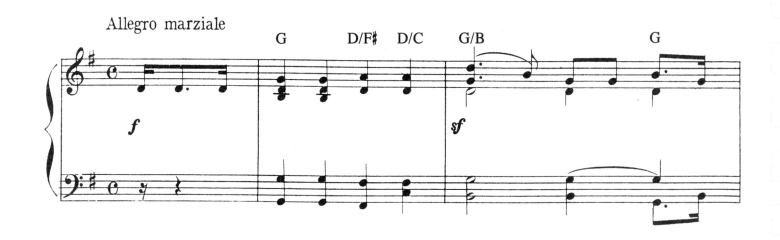

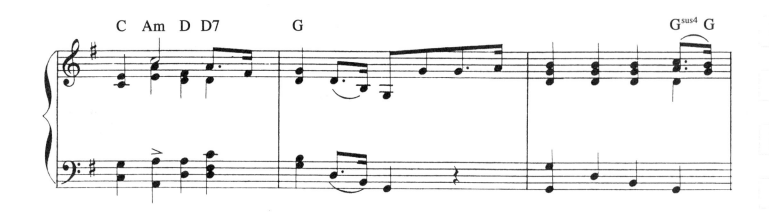

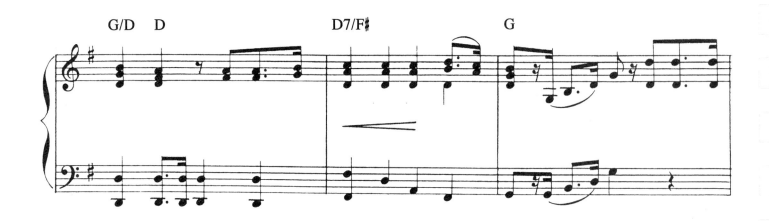

LASCIA CHI'O PIANGA
(from "Rinaldo")
By George Frederic Handel

LET THE BRIGHT SERAPHIM
(from "Samson")
By George Frederic Handel

LOCH LOMOND

Traditional Scottish Melody

LITTLE BROWN JUG

Traditional

Medium swing

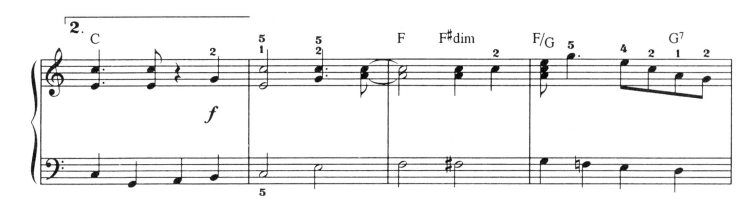

LONDONDERRY AIR

Traditional Irish

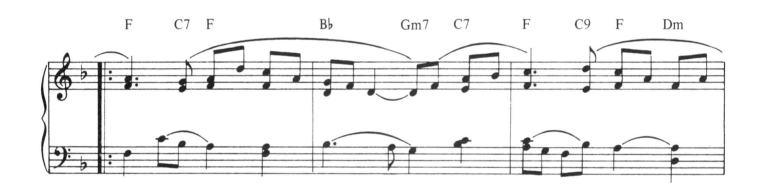

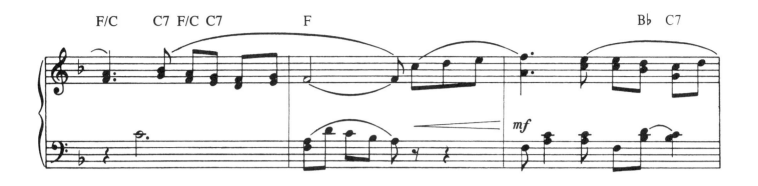

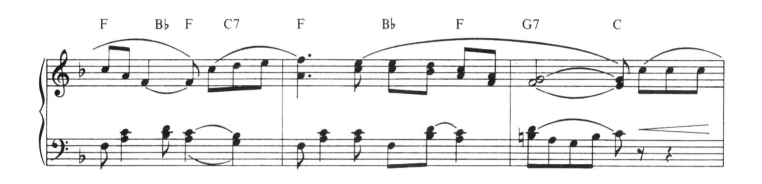

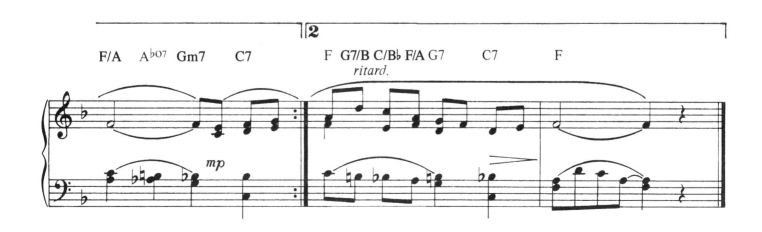

LUCK BE A LADY

(from "Guys and Dolls")

By Frank Loesser

158

MAKE YOURSELF COMFORTABLE

Words and Music by Bob Merrill

With a slow, gentle stomp (♩. = 82)

MERRY CHRISTMAS, MR. LAWRENCE
By RYUICHI SAKAMOTO

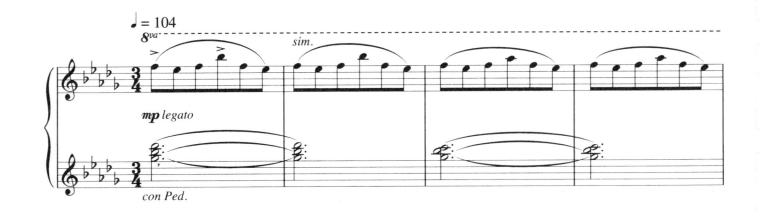

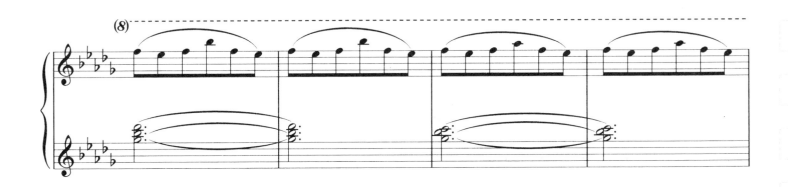

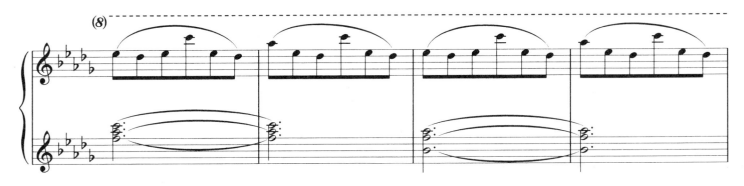

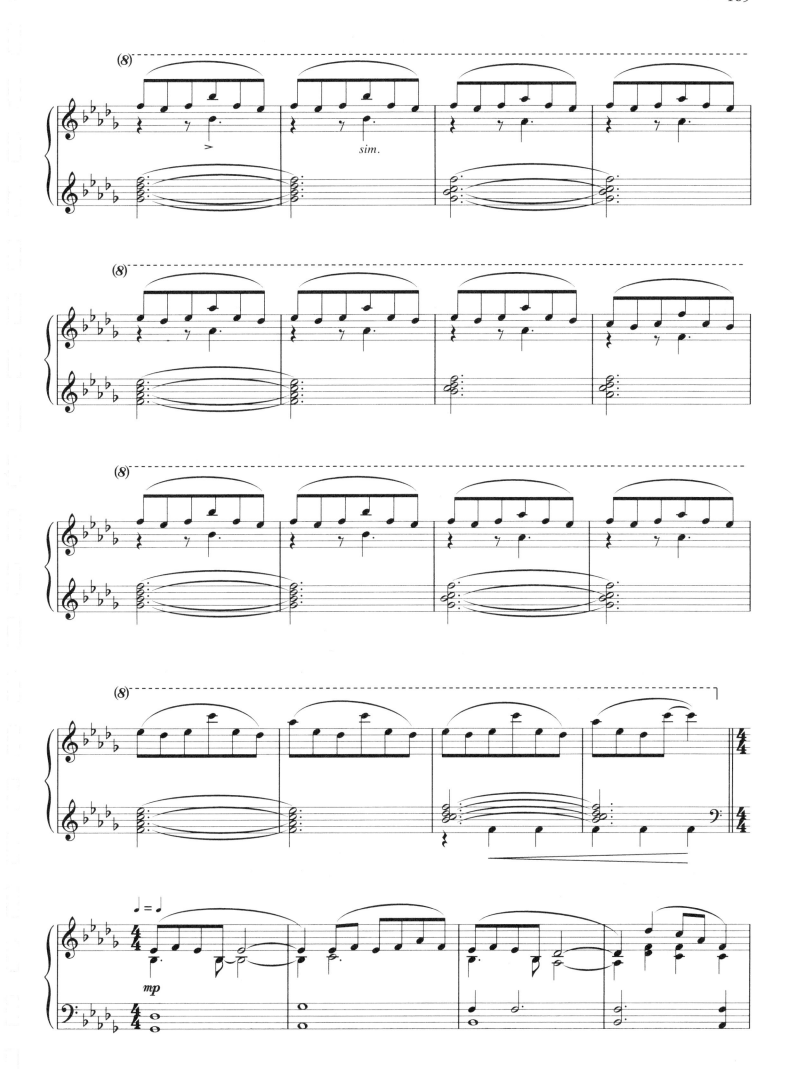

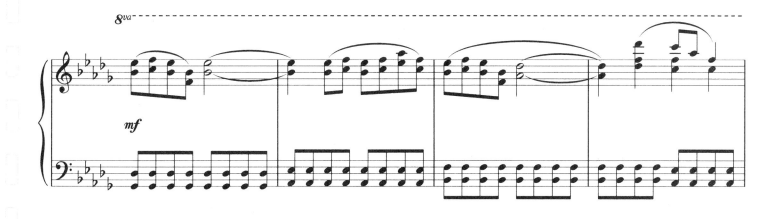

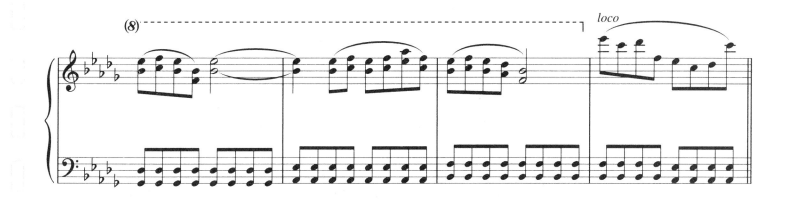

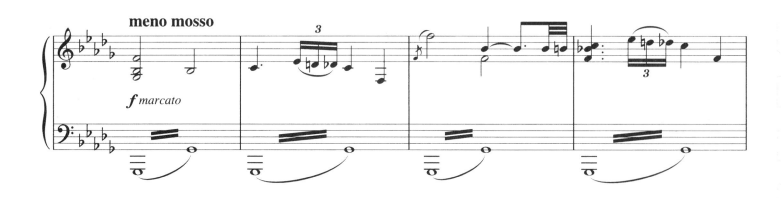

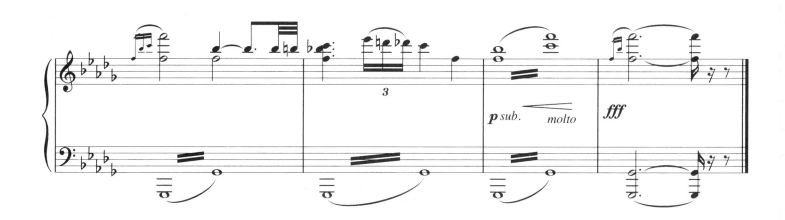

MICHAEL, ROW THE BOAT ASHORE

Traditional African-American

MIDNIGHT COWBOY
(Theme)

By JOHN BARRY

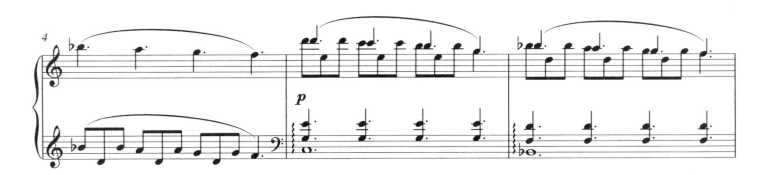

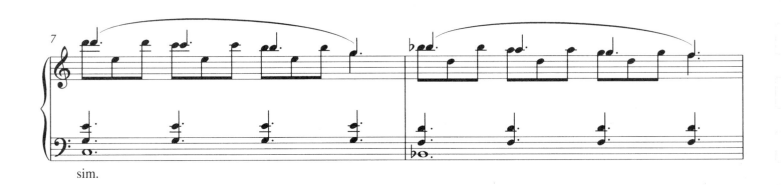

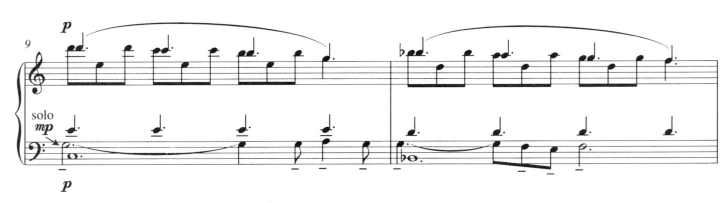

174

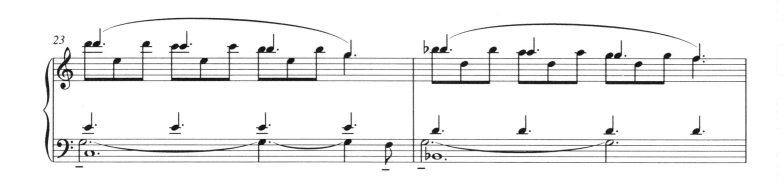

come prima

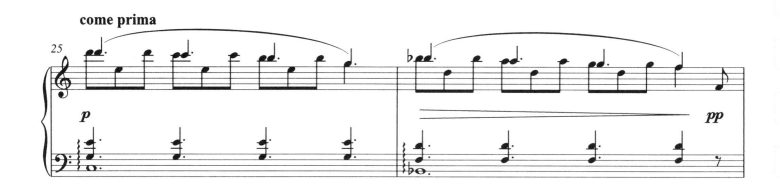

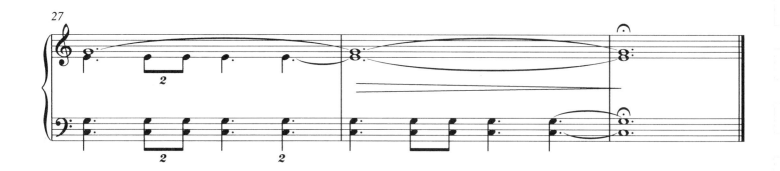

MY BONNIE LIES OVER THE OCEAN

Traditional Scottish

MINUET IN G MAJOR

By Ludwig van Beethoven

Allegretto (♩ = 120)

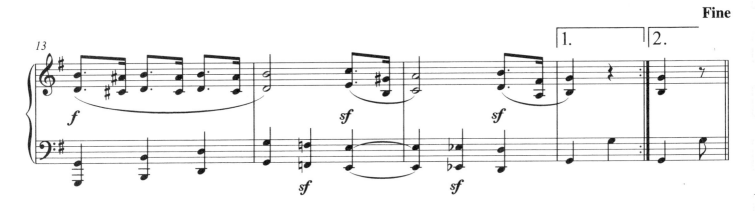

TRIO

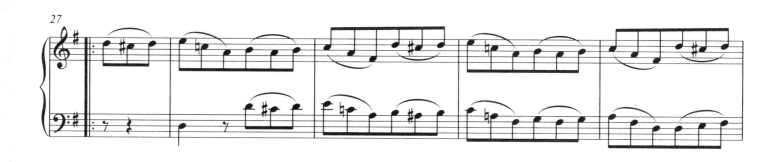

Minuet da capo

NIGHT TRAIN

Words by Oscar Washington and Lewis Simpkins
Music by Jimmy Forrest

THE NIGHT WE CALLED IT A DAY

Words by Tom Adair
Music by Matt Dennis

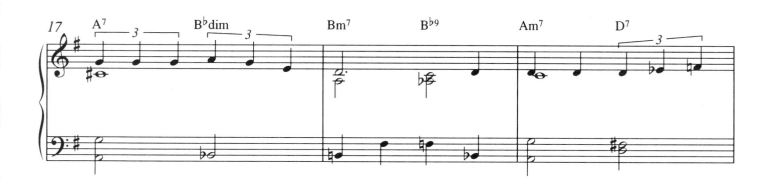
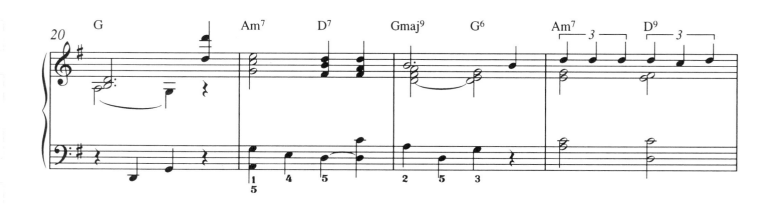
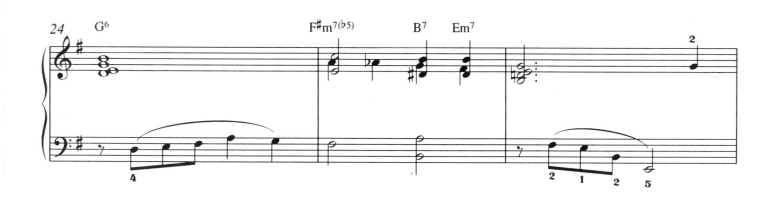

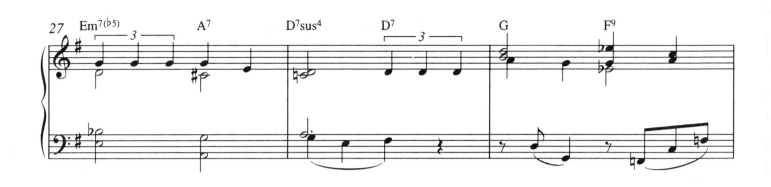

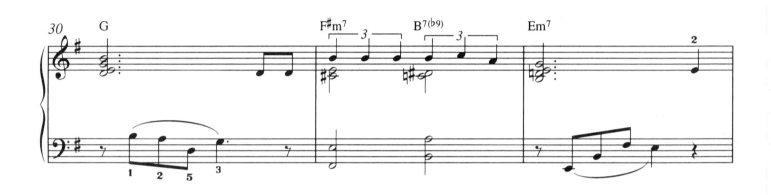

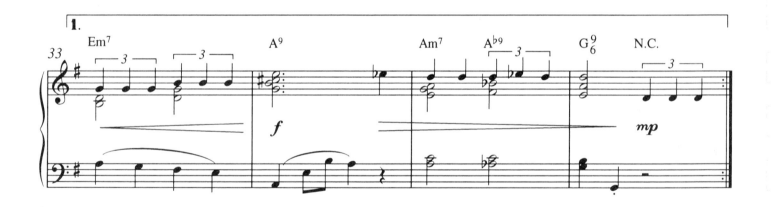

O TANNENBAUM
(O CHRISTMAS TREE)

Traditional German
Words by Ernst Anschuetz & Joachim August Zarnack

NOCTURNE IN F MINOR

By Frédéric Chopin

O COME, ALL YE FAITHFUL

Original Words and Music by John Francis Wade
English Words by Frederick Oakeley

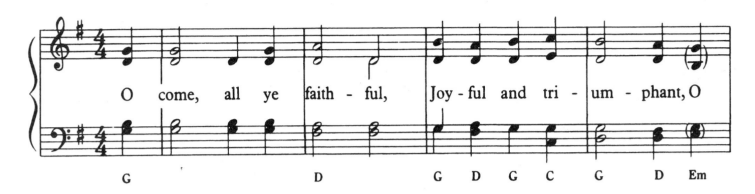

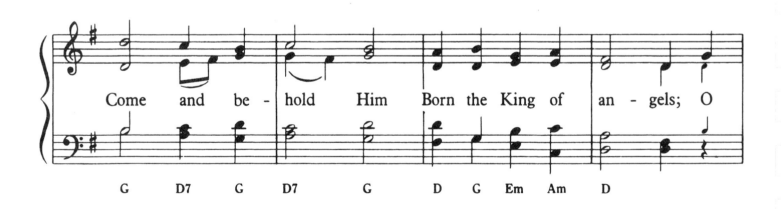

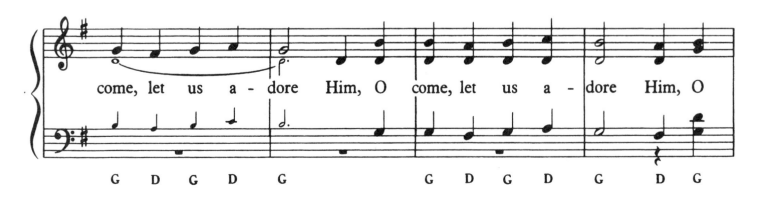

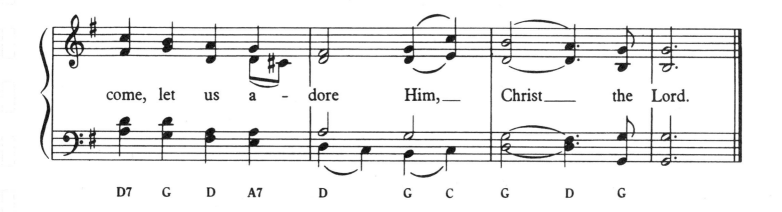

come, let us a - dore Him, — Christ — the Lord.

D7 G D A7 D G C G D G

2. God of God,
   Light of light,
   Lo! He abhors not the Virgin's womb;
   Very God,
   Begotten not created;

   O come, let us adore Him,
   O come, let us adore Him,
   O come, let us adore Him,
   Christ the Lord.

3. Sing, choirs of angels,
   Sing with exultation,
   Sing, all ye citizens of heaven above,
   Glory to God
   In the highest!

   O come, let us adore Him,
   O come, let us adore Him,
   O come, let us adore Him,
   Christ the Lord.

4. Yea, Lord, we greet Thee,
   Born this happy morning;
   Jesu, to Thee be glory given;
   Word of the Father,
   Now in flesh appearing;

   O come, let us adore Him,
   O come, let us adore Him,
   O come, let us adore Him,
   Christ the Lord.

O SUSANNA

Words and Music by Stephen Collins Foster

ON TOP OF OLD SMOKEY

Traditional American

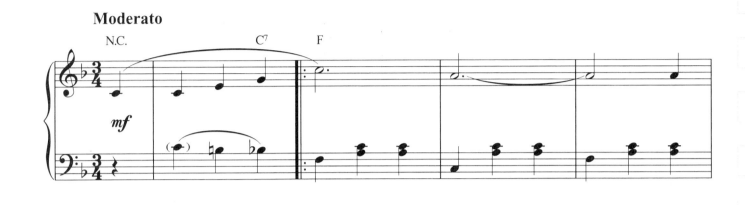

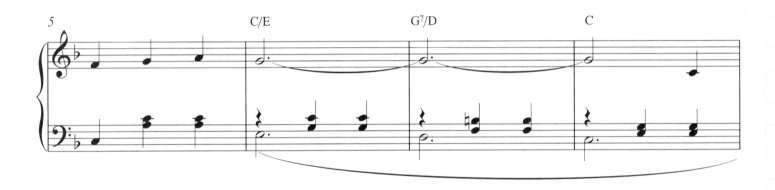

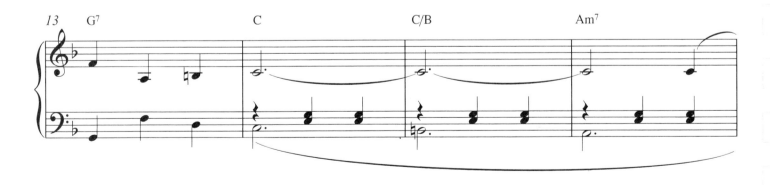

ONE NOTE SAMBA

Original Words by Newton Mendonca
Music by Antonio Carlos Jobim

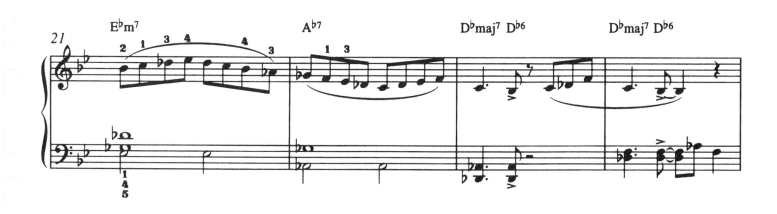

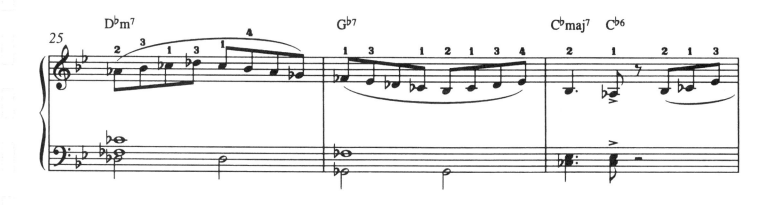

196

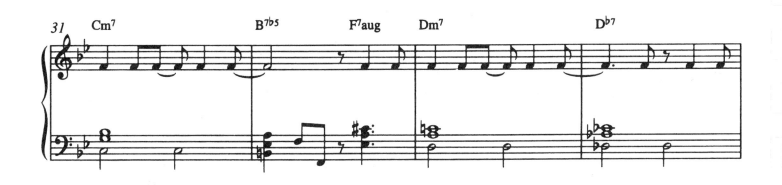

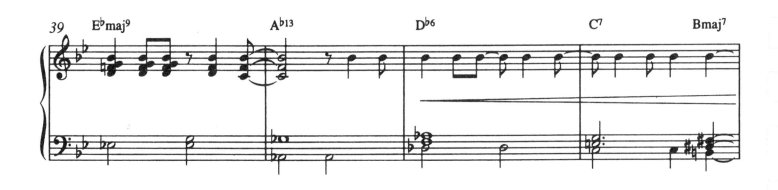

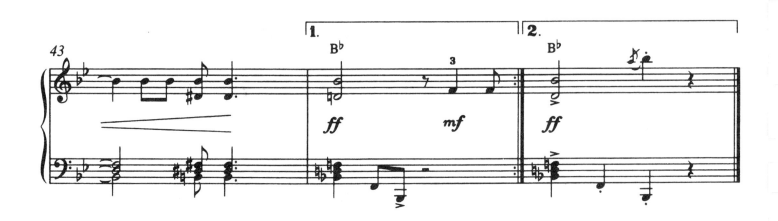

ONCE IN A ROYAL DAVID'S CITY

Words by Cecil Alexander
Music by Henry Gauntlett

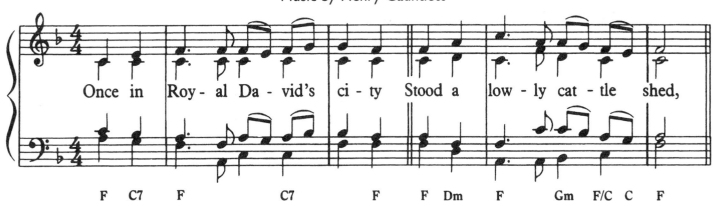

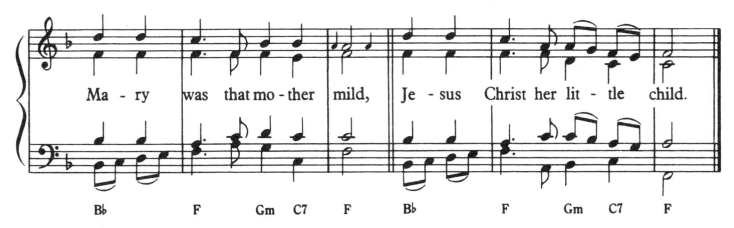

2. He came down to earth from heaven
    Who is God and Lord of all,
And his shelter was a stable,
    And his cradle was a stall;
With the poor and mean and lowly
Lived on earth our Saviour holy.

3. And through all his wondrous childhood
    He would honour and obey,
Love and watch the lowly Maiden,
    In whose gentle arms he lay:
Christian children all must be,
Mild, obedient, good as he.

4. And our eyes at last shall see him,
    Through his own redeeming love,
For that Child so dear and gentle
    Is our Lord in heaven above;
And he leads his children on
To the place where he is gone.

5. Not in that poor lowly stable,
    With the oxen standing by,
We shall see him; but in heaven,
    Set at God's right hand on high;
Where like stars his children crowned
All in white shall wait around.

PASSAGE OF TIME

(from "Chocolot")

By Rachel Portman

200

PELAGIA'S SONG
(from "Captain Corelli's Mandolin")
By Stephen Warbeck

PIANO CONCERTO NO. 5
(2nd Movement)
By Johann Sebastian Bach

PRELUDE IN C MAJOR

By Johann Sebastian Bach

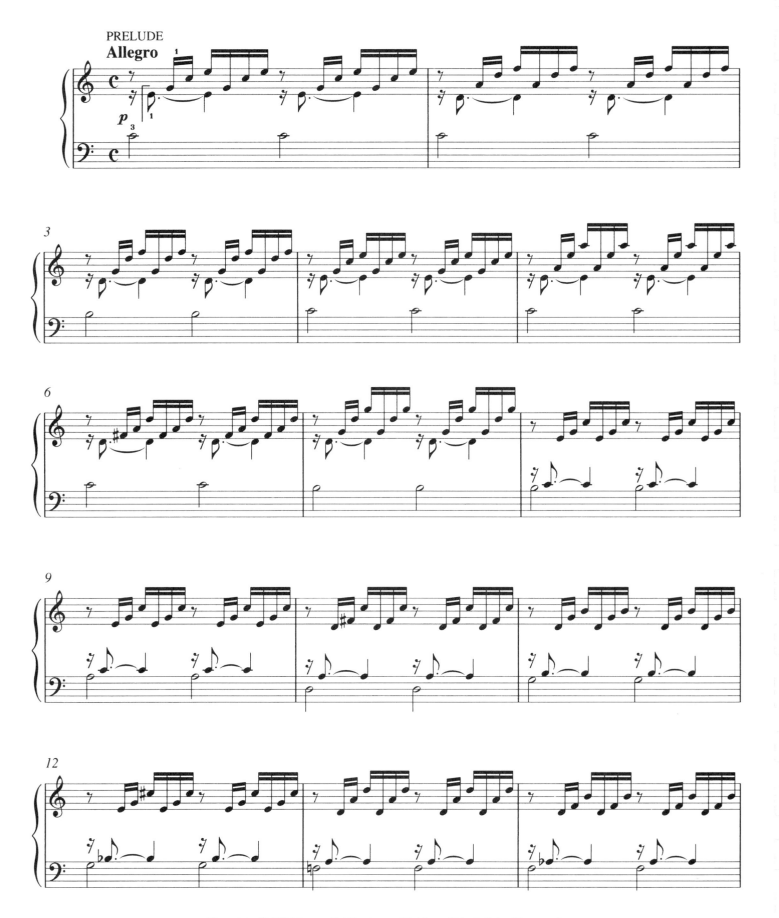

PRELUDE IN Db MAJOR
'RAINDROP'
(Op. 28, No. 15)

By Frédéric Chopin

Andante sostenuto

con pedale

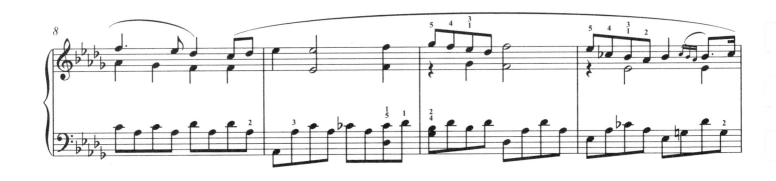

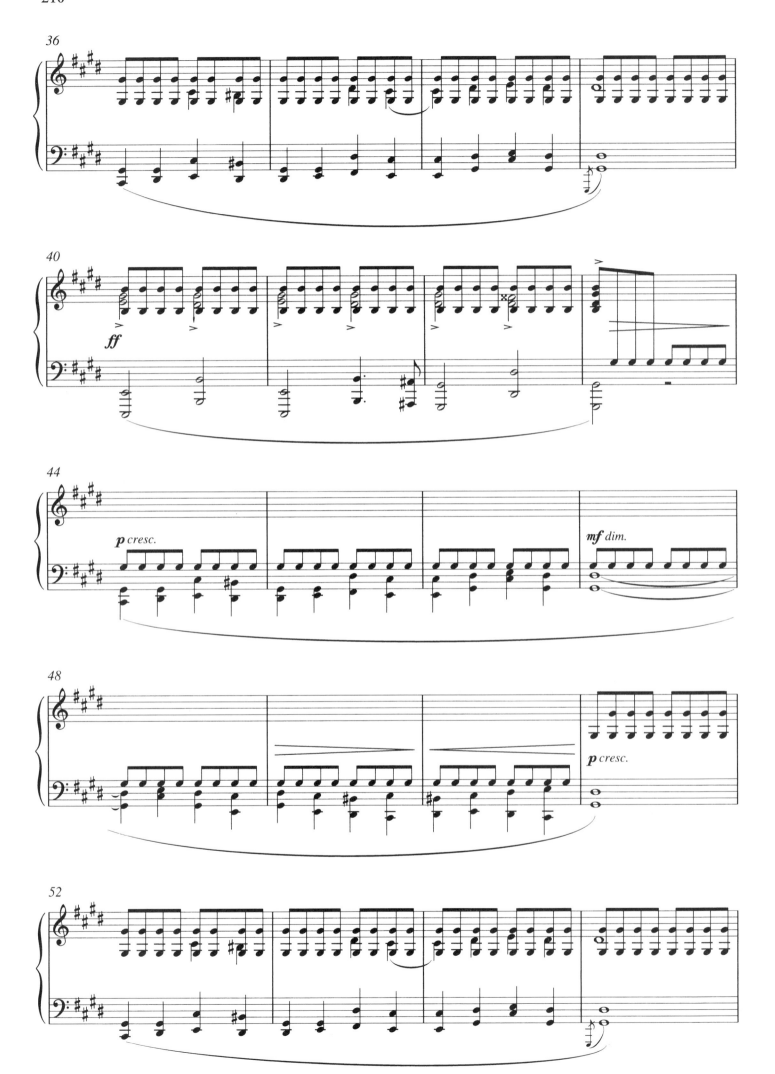

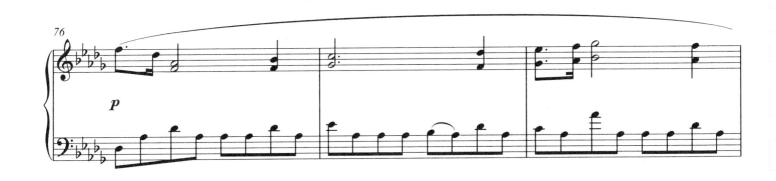

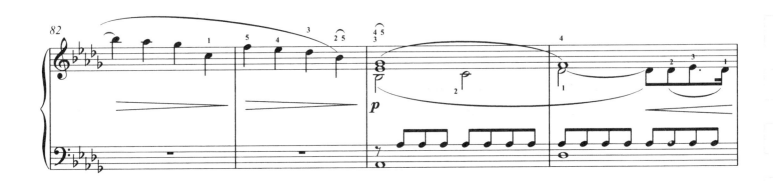

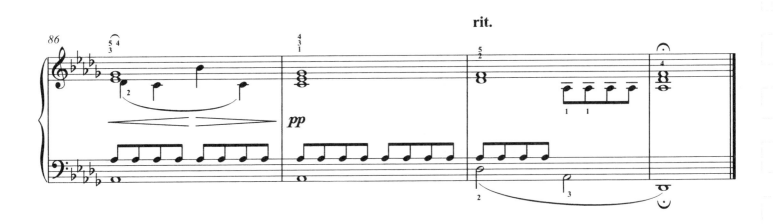

PIZZICATO POLKA
(from "Sylvia")
Composed by Leo Delibes

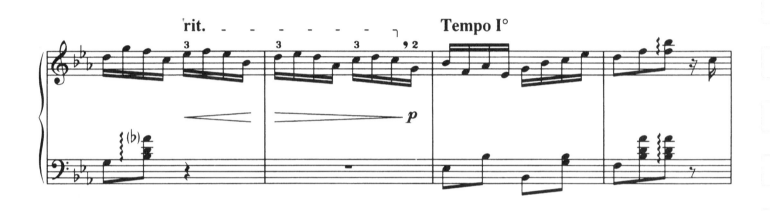

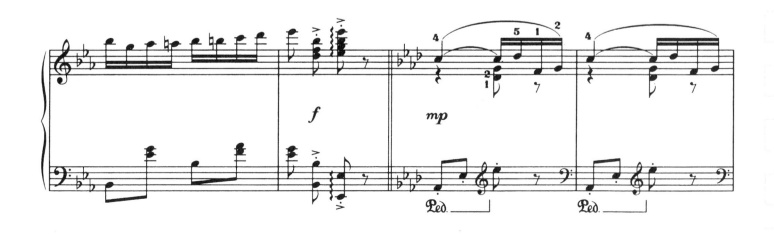

PRELUDE IN E MINOR
(Op. 28, No. 4)

By Frédéric Chopin

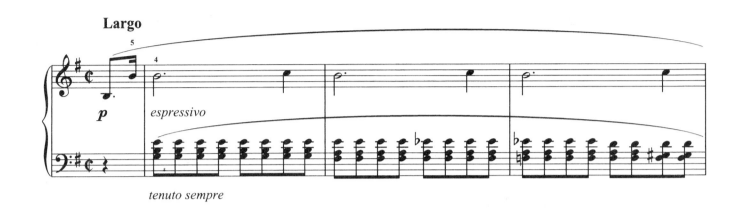

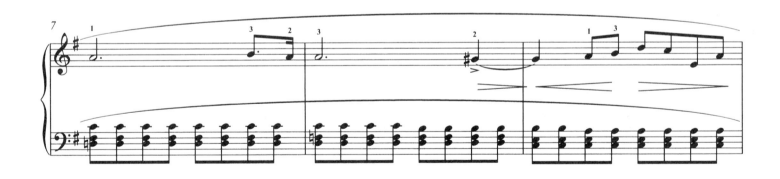

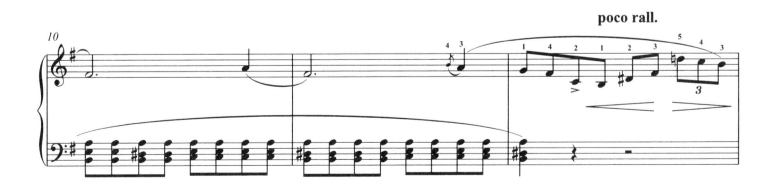

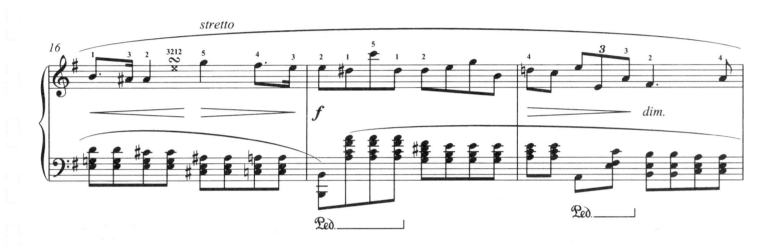

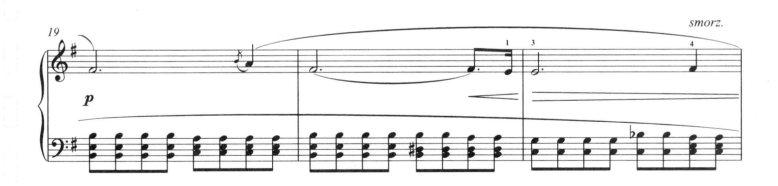

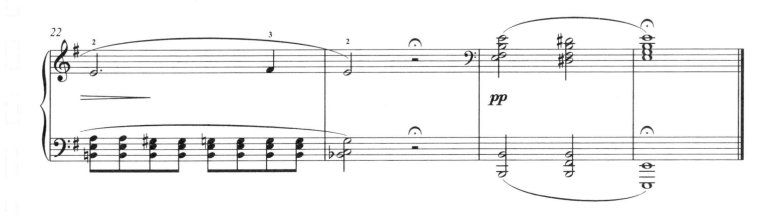

QUIET NIGHTS OF QUIET STARS

English Words by Gene Lees
Original Words and Music by Antonio Carlos Jobim

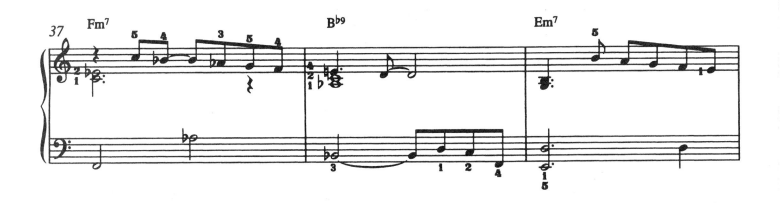

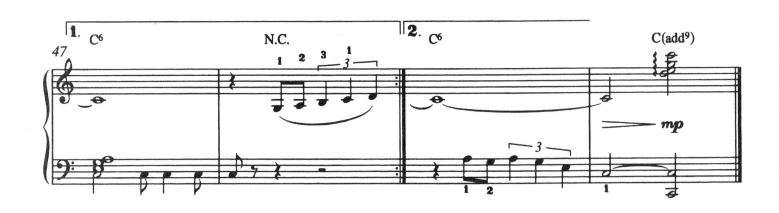

SATIN DOLL

Music by Duke Ellington, Words by Billy Strayhorn and Johnny Mercer

RAIDER'S MARCH

(from the Paramount Motion Picture "Raiders Of The Lost Ark")

Music by John Williams

With movement

226

SAILING

By Gavin Sutherland

THE SAILOR'S HORNPIPE

Traditional English
Arranged by Barrie Carson Turner

SCARBOROUGH FAIR

Traditional

SERENADE IN B♭
'GRAN PARTITA'

By Wolfgang Amadeus Mozart

SHE'LL BE COMING ROUND THE MOUNTAIN

Traditional American

SILENT NIGHT

Words by Joseph Mohr
Music by Franz Grüber

2. Silent night, holy night,
   Shepherds wake at the sight;
   Glory streams from heaven afar,
   Heavenly hosts sing Alleluia.
   Christ the Saviour is born!
   Christ the Saviour is born!

3. Silent night, holy night,
   Son of God, love's pure light;
   Radiance beams from Thy holy face,
   With the dawn of redeeming grace,
   Jesus, Lord at Thy birth,
   Jesus, Lord at Thy birth.

SONATA IN G MAJOR
(Op. 49, No. 2, 2nd Movement)
By Ludwig van Beethoven

Tempo di Menuetto

SLEEPERS AWAKE
(from "Cantata No. 140")
By Johann Sebastian Bach

Allegretto tranquillo

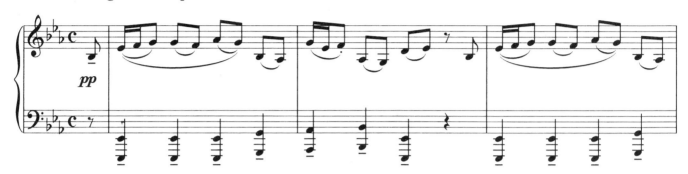

simile

sempre **pp**

SOLITUDE

By DUKE ELLINGTON, EDDIE DE LANGE and IRVING MILLS

SYMPHONY NO. 7
(Allegretto Theme)

By Ludwig van Beethoven

STEAL AWAY

Traditional African-American

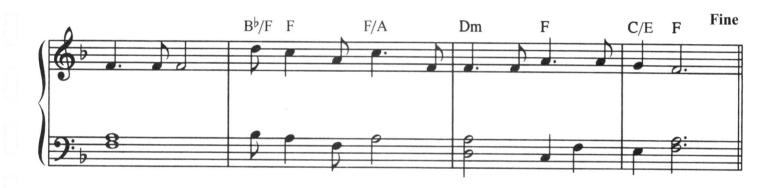

SWING LOW, SWEET CHARIOT

Traditional African-American

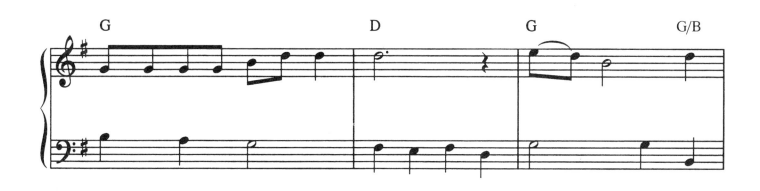

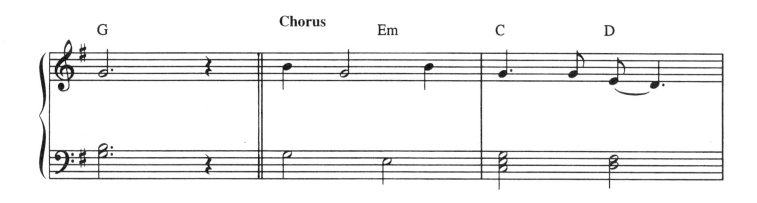

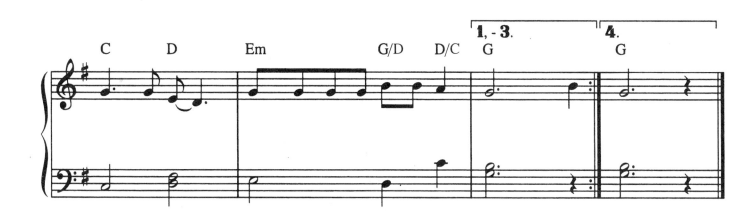

THAT OLE DEVIL CALLED LOVE

Words and Music by DORIS FISHER and ALLAN ROBERTS

260

261

THEME FROM E.T.
(THE EXTRA-TERRESTRIAL)

Music by JOHN WILLIAMS

Moderato

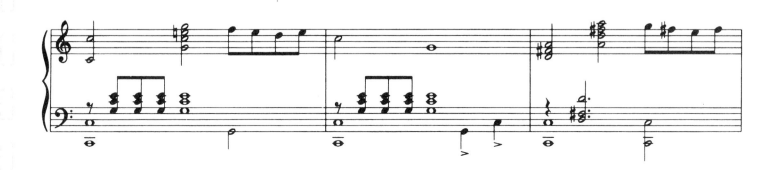

THE GODFATHER (LOVE THEME)
(From the Paramount Picture "The Godfather")
By Nino Rota

THIS YEAR'S LOVE

Words and Music by DAVID GRAY

TOM DOOLEY

Traditional American

TROUT QUINTET
(Op. 114, 4th Movement)

By Franz Schubert

UN BEL DiVEDREMO

(from "Madame Butterfly")

By Giacomo Puccini

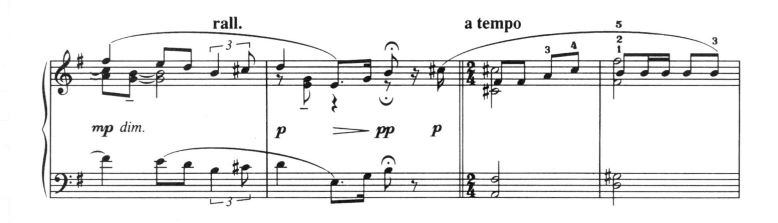

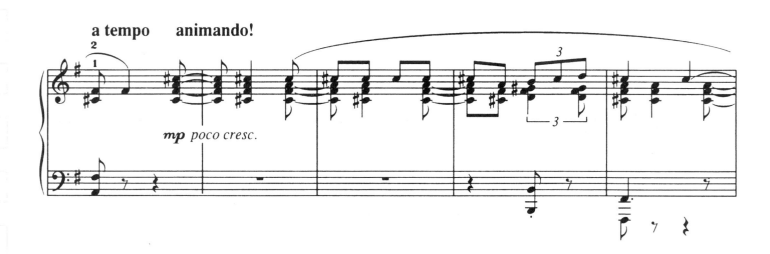

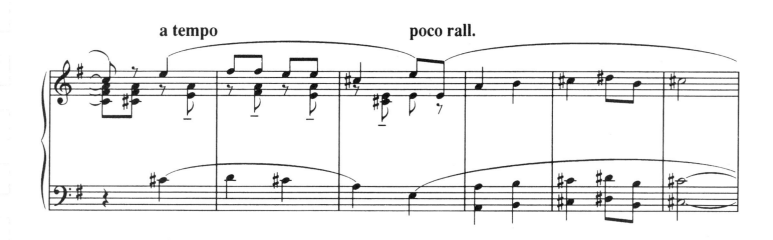

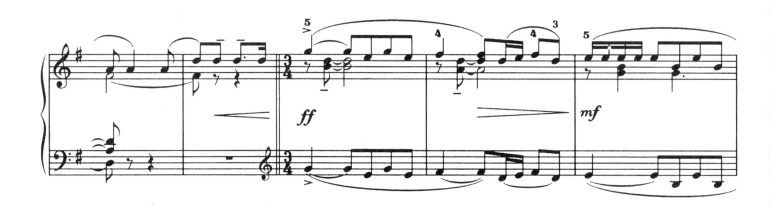

VOI CHE SAPETE
(from "The Marriage of Figaro")
By Wolfgang Amadeus Mozart

WALTZ OF THE FLOWERS
(from "The Nutcracker Suite")

By Peter Ilyich Tchaikovsky

Very freely and held back

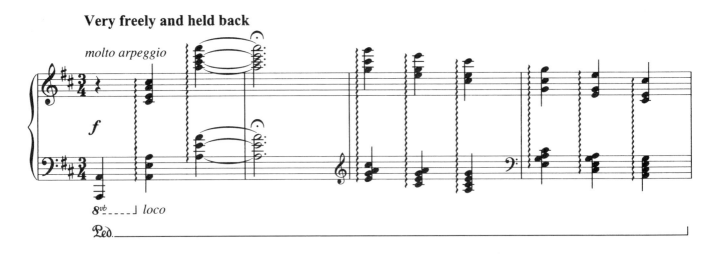

a tempo di valse moderato

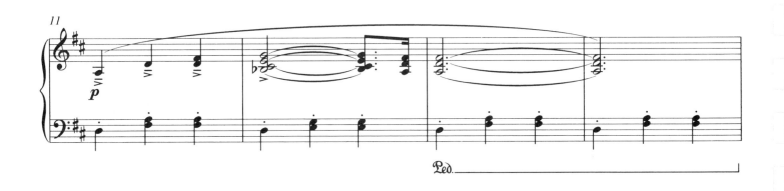

WE WISH YOU A MERRY CHRISTMAS

Traditional

2. Now bring us some figgy pudding,
Now bring us some figgy pudding,
Now bring us some figgy pudding,
And bring some out here.

Good tidings we bring
To you and your kin,
We wish you a Merry Christmas,
And a Happy New Year.

3. For we all like figgy pudding,
We all like figgy pudding,
For we all like figgy pudding,
So bring some out here.

4. And we won't go till we've got some,
We won't go, till we've got some,
And we won't go till we've got some,
So bring some out here.

WHEN JOHNNY COMES MARCHING HOME

Words by Katherine Purvis & Music by James Milton Black

Lively march tempo

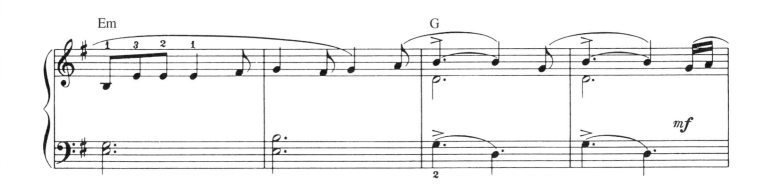

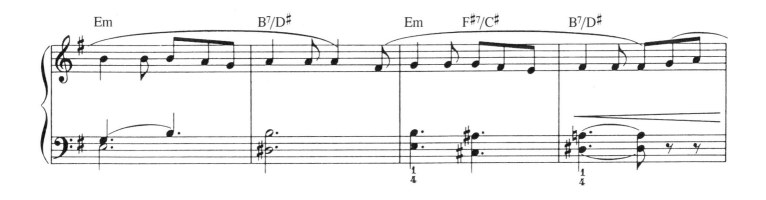

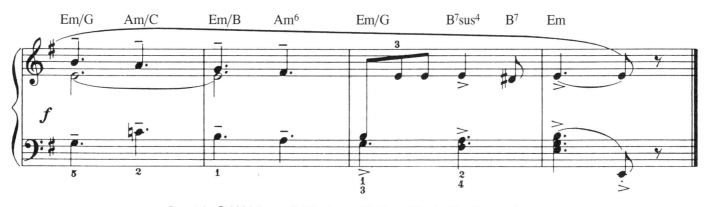

WHEN SUNNY GETS BLUE

Lyric by Jack Segal
Music by Marvin Fisher

WHEN THE SAINTS GO MARCHING IN

Traditional

Moderato

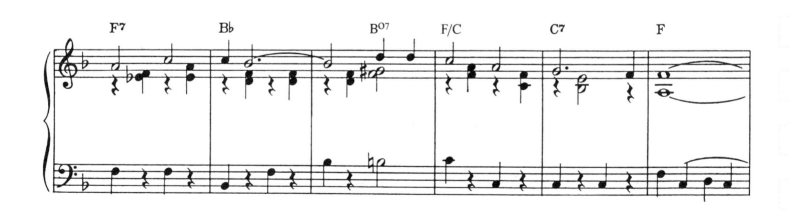

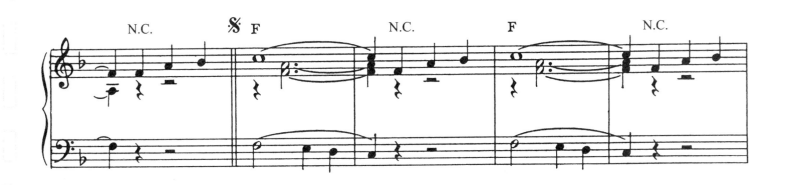

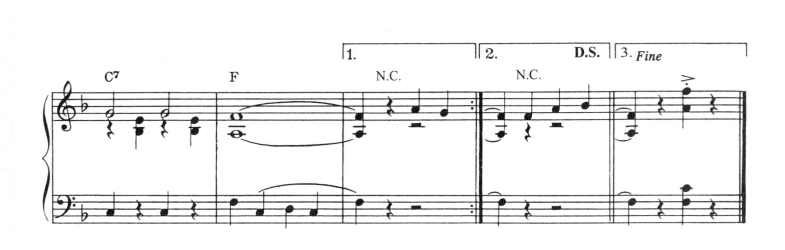

WHILE SHEPHERDS WATCHED

Music: Traditional
Words by Nahum Tate

2. "Fear not," said he; For mighty dread
   Had seized their troubled mind;
"Glad tidings of great joy I bring
   To you and all mankind."

3. "To you in David's town this day
   Is born of David's line
A Saviour, Who is Christ the Lord;
   And this shall be the sign:"

4. "The heavenly Babe you there shall find
   To human view display'd,
All meanly wrapp'd in swathing bands,
   And in a manger laid."

5. Thus spake the seraph; and forthwith
   Appear'd a shining throng
Of Angels praising God, who thus
   Address'd their joyful song:

6. "All glory be to God on high,
   And to the earth be peace;
Good-will henceforth from heaven to men
   Begin and never cease."

WHEN YOU SAY NOTHING AT ALL

Words and Music by Paul Overstreet and Don Schlitz

THE YELLOW ROSE OF TEXAS

Traditional American

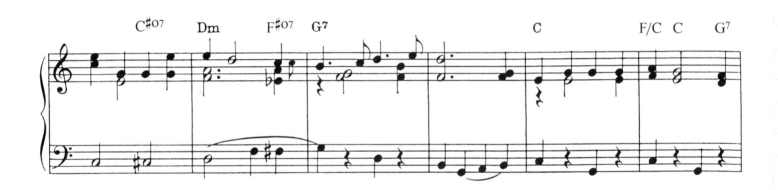

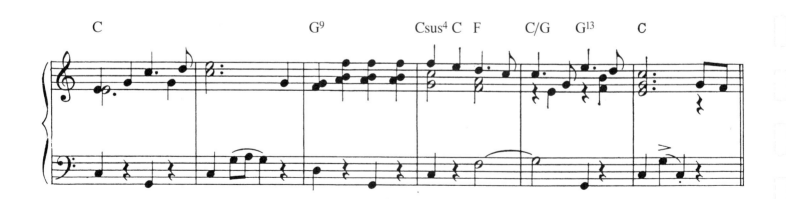

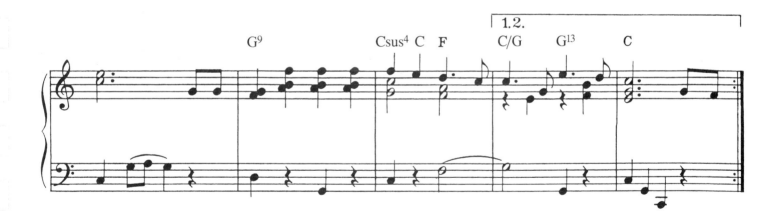

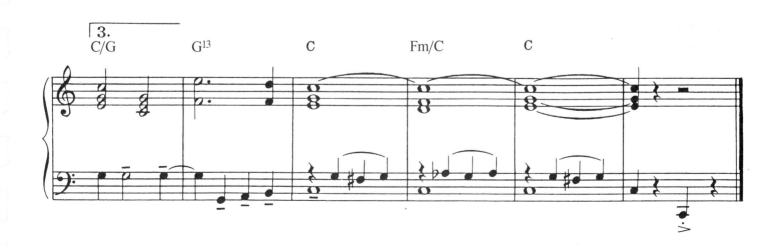

YANKEE DOODLE

Traditional American